People of the Ancient World

THE ANCIENT CHINESE

WRITTEN BY

VIRGINIA SCHOMP

Franklin Watts
A Division of Scholastic Inc.
New York Toronto London Auckland Sydney
Mexico City New Delhi Hong Kong
Danbury, Connecticut

To my brother Bob,
who deserves a book all his own

Note to readers: Definitions for words in **bold** can be found in the Glossary at the back of this book.

"The Lament of Hsi-chün" (page 82) is reprinted from *A Hundred and Seventy Chinese Poems,* translated by Arthur Waley. (New York: Alfred A. Knopf, 1918.)

Photographs © 2004: Art Resource, NY: 30, 31 (Werner Forman), 20, 26, 90 bottom left (Giraudon/Bibliotheque Nationale, Paris, France), 81 (Erich Lessing/National Museum, Beijing); Bridgeman Art Library International Ltd., London/New York: 16 (Bibliotheque Nationale, Paris, France), 6 (British Museum, London, UK), 78, 79 (Christies Images/Private Collection), 91 top, 97 center top (Museum of Fine Arts, Boston, MA, USA/Denman Waldo Ross Collection), 13, 93 bottom, 95 center (National Palace Museum, Taipei, Taiwan); Corbis Images: 7, 22, 53, 56, 58 (Asian Art & Archaeology, Inc.), 63 (Charles & Josette Lenars), 69 (Liu Liqun), 38, 39 (Royal Ontario Musem); FeatureChina.com: 60 (Ruan Banhui), 54, 55 (Zhao Hang), 32 (Long Woo); Getty Images/Chai Hin Goh/AFP Photo: 50, 90 top right; Index Stock Imagery/Keren Su: 64, 65; Landov, LLC: 4 center, 15, 21, 42, 75, 83, 86, 91 bottom, 92 bottom left, 97 top, 97 bottom; Lonely Planet Images/Martin Moos: 37, 90 top left, 95 top; National Geographic Image Collection/O. Louis Mazzatenta: 9, 76; Science Museum, Science & Society Picture Library: 97 center bottom; The Art Archive/Picture Desk: 46, 47, 92 bottom center (Freer Gallery of Art), 27 (Dagli Orti/Musee Guimet, Paris), 90 bottom right, 96 (The British Library); The Image Works: 88, 89 (John Nordell), 67 (Panorama Images), 35, 68, 70, 92 bottom right (Topham-HIP/Science Museum, London), 85 (Topham-HIP/The British Museum); William Lindesay/The National Museum of Chinese History: 29, 44, 62, 77.

Library of Congress Cataloging-in-Publication Data

Schomp, Virginia.
  The ancient Chinese / by Virginia Schomp.
  p. cm. — (People of the ancient world)
  "Simultaneously published in Canada."
  Audience: Ages 11-13.
Includes bibliographical references and index.
ISBN 0-531-11817-7 (lib. bdg.)   0-531-16737-2 (pbk.)
1. China—Civilization—Juvenile literature. I. Title. II. Series.
DS721.53677 2004
931—dc22
                                                    2004002174

Contents

AT THE CENTER OF THE WORLD

Ancient Chinese texts speak of a golden age of riches, power, and accomplishment thousands of years in the country's past. Modern historians once thought that those stories were myths.

Then, in the early 1900s, scientists studying mysterious animal bones unearthed in northern China made a remarkable discovery. Faded markings on the bones were the **inscriptions** of fortune-telling priests, or **oracles**, who lived more than 3,500 years ago. Further explorations uncovered buried palaces, tombs, workshops, and beautiful bronze weapons and vessels. China's legendary past was a reality. In fact, we now know that the history of China dates back some 4,000 years, making it the world's oldest surviving civilization.

An oracle bone was carved with messages from the gods. This bone dates back to the Shang dynasty.

Throughout most of their long history, the Chinese people viewed the outside world with a mixture of curiosity and contempt. They often adopted new ideas and useful technologies from other cultures. At the same time, they thought of outsiders as uncivilized "barbarians." That attitude was reflected in the name the ancient Chinese gave their vast homeland. They called it Zhongguo, or the "Middle Kingdom," because they believed that it was the center of the civilized world.

The Middle Kingdom's earliest settlements were small farming villages along the banks of two rivers: the Huang He (also called the Yellow River) in the north and the Chang Jiang (or Yangtze River) in the south. Over time these settlements grew into states. Rival states fought over control of territory, and the kings of the stronger states ruled the lands and people they conquered. Powerful families passed down control of their kingdoms from generation to generation. China's history is divided into periods named for these ruling families, or dynasties.

According to legend, the Xia (shah) family founded China's first **dynasty** in 2205 B.C. However, the Xia left few lasting traces of their civilization.

The first dynasty for which we have solid evidence is the Shang, which came to power sometime around 1700 B.C. The Shang people created elaborately decorated bronze vessels and other objects. They developed the earliest known Chinese writing, the markings on the "oracle bones." These inscriptions were believed to relay messages from the gods, sent to help the kings rule wisely and well. But even divine advice could not ensure eternal power. In 1046 B.C. the Zhou (joh) family rebelled against the Shang and stormed their capital, forcing their last king to commit suicide.

Like the Shang kings, the Zhou divided the Middle Kingdom into states, which were ruled by members of the royal family.

These great lords became increasingly strong and independent. Toward the end of Zhou rule, in the two chaotic centuries known as the Warring States period, the lords of the seven largest states fought a series of bloody battles. Finally, the western state of Qin (sometimes spelled Ch'in) triumphed over all the others.

In 221 B.C. the king of Qin took a grand new title: Shi Huangdi (shir hwong-dee), or "First Magnificent Emperor." The dynasty

This statue of an archer was discovered in the tomb of Qin Shi Huangdi, along with thousands of other clay warriors.

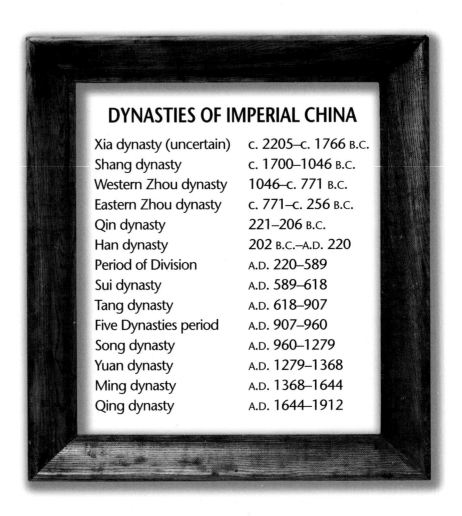

DYNASTIES OF IMPERIAL CHINA

Xia dynasty (uncertain)	c. 2205–c. 1766 B.C.
Shang dynasty	c. 1700–1046 B.C.
Western Zhou dynasty	1046–c. 771 B.C.
Eastern Zhou dynasty	c. 771–c. 256 B.C.
Qin dynasty	221–206 B.C.
Han dynasty	202 B.C.–A.D. 220
Period of Division	A.D. 220–589
Sui dynasty	A.D. 589–618
Tang dynasty	A.D. 618–907
Five Dynasties period	A.D. 907–960
Song dynasty	A.D. 960–1279
Yuan dynasty	A.D. 1279–1368
Ming dynasty	A.D. 1368–1644
Qing dynasty	A.D. 1644–1912

founded by Qin Shi Huangdi marked the beginning of a new era, when all the land was united under a single all-powerful ruler. It also gave us our name for that land, China.

The Qin dynasty survived only a few years. Other dynasties and other powerful emperors followed. In fact, China's **imperial** age lasted more than two thousand years, until A.D. 1912. Under the emperors the country saw periods of war and chaos, peace and accomplishment. The people of ancient China built some of the world's largest cities and most ambitious engineering projects. They created fine literature and exquisite arts and crafts.

Their philosophies, inventions, and advances in science and technology amazed and transformed the world.

How do we know so much about China's long history? Most of our information comes from the ancient Chinese themselves. From a very early age, they kept written records on bone, stone, bronze, silk, and paper. They also buried their dead with objects for use in the next world, including coins, weapons, tools, clothing, jewelry, and even food and drink. To modern-day **archaeologists,** these remains of an ancient culture are seen as evidence. Like

A team of archaeologists excavates a graveyard from the Shang dynasty.

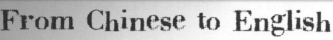

From Chinese to English

Translating Chinese into English has always been a challenge for scholars. Different sources have often spelled the same name different ways. In 1979 China's government adopted a new system called Pinyin for translating the names of people and places. In most cases Pinyin spells names close to the way they are pronounced in English. We have used Pinyin throughout this book. For names that are especially difficult, we have added pronunciation guides in parentheses after the word.

detectives investigating a baffling case, archaeologists examine the ancient records. They read texts that have been handed down from generation to generation, copied and recopied over thousands of years. They dig up the ruins of tombs and settlements in search of long-buried treasures. Studying and comparing all these sources, they piece together pictures of what life was like in China's distant past.

Today archaeologists are still at work unlocking the mysteries of ancient China. Their findings take us to exciting places and introduce us to extraordinary people. They create a link between past and present, helping us understand this ancient culture's contributions to our modern world. Most importantly, learning about the ancient Chinese helps us discover the many things we have in common with the people of a culture distant from our own. And that can enrich our understanding of all humanity.

Chapter I

KINGS AND EMPERORS

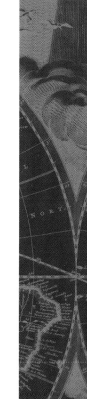

China's emperor Kublai Khan (koo-bluh kahn) was "the most powerful man since Adam," wrote Venetian merchant-traveler Marco Polo around A.D. 1300. Polo spent nearly twenty years in the emperor's service. After he returned home, he wrote an account of his adventures. *The Travels of Marco Polo* gave Europeans their first glimpse of the fabulous treasures and culture of China's imperial court.

Polo described Kublai Khan's palace as "the most extensive that has ever yet been known." Inside this magnificent estate the emperor was surrounded by a "personal guard . . . of twelve thousand horsemen." Hundreds of young women "distinguished for beauty of features and fairness of complexion" attended to his every need. Adding to the emperor's wealth were gifts from "the people of every kingdom and province throughout his dominions." During one lavish festival, more than five thousand camels and elephants carried "valuable presents of gold, silver, and precious stones." After the "Great Khan" reviewed this "pleasing spectacle," he and his guests enjoyed a splendid feast. "On this occasion," Polo wrote, "a lion is led into the presence of his Majesty, one so tame that it is taught to lay itself down at his feet."

In Marco Polo's day most readers scoffed at these fantastic tales. Modern historians believe that some of the Venetian's stories were invented or greatly exaggerated but that many others were true. Whether or not it is completely accurate, *The Travels of Marco Polo* gives us a fascinating picture of the grandeur of an emperor's court.

Sons of Heaven

Kublai Khan was China's 123rd emperor and the founder of the Yuan dynasty of **Mongol** rulers. Mongol warriors had conquered

The Message of the Bones

When a Shang king was worried about the future, he turned to his long-dead ancestors. First he had his royal oracle scratch a question on a polished ox bone. He might ask, "The king is going to conduct a military campaign. Will he be protected?" Then the royal priest touched the back of the bone with a red-hot poker. Cracks appeared around the question.

The king and priest interpreted the pattern of the cracks to read the spirits' answer: "yes," "no," or "undecided."

Through the inscriptions on the oracle bones, archaeologists have worked out a history of the Shang rulers: their plans, deeds, hopes, and fears. After three thousand years these ancient bones are still carrying messages to a distant world.

Kublai Khan, founder of the Yuan dynasty, is shown at a hunt. The emperor is wearing a white fur coat and riding a black horse.

all of China by A.D. 1279. The Chinese bitterly resented their "barbarian" masters. To win his subjects' acceptance, Kublai Khan adopted Chinese traditions that reached back to the days of the Middle Kingdom's earliest kings.

Three thousand years before the Yuan, the people of the Shang dynasty had believed that their kings were exalted beings whose power came directly from heaven. Only the king could communicate with the spirit world. Through holy rituals, including human and animal sacrifices, he won the favor of the all-powerful gods of nature. The king also received help and guidance from the wise spirits of his ancestors, through the oracle bones.

When the Zhou overthrew the Shang in 1046 B.C., they knew that the people of the Middle Kingdom would be frightened. Who would communicate with the gods and keep order in the world? The Zhou had a comforting answer. They said that the last Shang king was so weak and corrupt that he had lost the "Mandate of Heaven"—the god-given right to rule. The gods had given the mandate to the Zhou kings instead, making them the true "Sons of Heaven."

This was a revolutionary new idea. It meant that no dynasty could ever claim the right to eternal power. The gods would support a king only as long as he ruled justly and virtuously, taking good care of the lands and people entrusted to him. If he proved unworthy, heaven would remove its mandate, so that the people could rise up and overthrow him.

From this point on, every one of China's kings and emperors claimed the Mandate of Heaven. With that divine gift came grave responsibilities, along with authority and glory.

During the Zhou dynasty, emperors began to call themselves Sons of Heaven. As long as an emperor was wise and just, the heavenly spirits would support his right to the throne.

A Tradition of Majesty

The Sons of Heaven were the chosen of the gods. That set them far apart from ordinary mortals. Every aspect of their lives reflected their unique and awesome role.

An emperor lived in the innermost part of a grand palace, attended by a host of guards, servants, and advisers. In later imperial times the splendors of the imperial court were legendary. Every luxury was at the emperor's fingertips. His every command was instantly obeyed. With a wave of his hand he could make a beggar a prince or sentence thousands of innocent men to a lifetime of hard labor.

Sharing the pleasures of the court were the emperor's wives. These included his legal wife, the empress, plus hundreds or thousands of "secondary wives," or **concubines**. The duty of these pampered ladies of the court was to ensure the emperor's happiness and provide him with sons. The mother of a son who was appointed crown prince (the person next in line to the throne) could rise to the rank of empress.

Along with the privileges of court life, the emperor had solemn duties. As the Son of Heaven, he was responsible for the well-being of all the people. Much of his time was spent presiding over long court ceremonies and religious rituals. He approved government policies, issued decrees, and received ambassadors bearing **tribute** from conquered lands. He offered prayers and sacrifices to the gods and ancestors. His performance of all these duties ensured the empire's strength and heaven's continued blessings.

Power and majesty followed the Sons of Heaven to the grave. Thousands of workers labored for years constructing an emperor's lavish tomb. Filled with both practical goods and priceless luxuries, this underground empire re-created a ruler's living world. It ensured that the departed emperor would be comfortable and contented when he took his place among the spirits of his ancestors.

While an emperor enjoyed many luxuries, his life was not all pleasure. He had to manage the country and take care of foreign affairs.

A Glorious Age

Qin Shi Huangdi, often called the First Emperor, was a brilliant but brutal ruler. He united the warring states of China and established standard forms of writing, money, and weights and measures. According to some accounts, he also burned books, outlawed scholarship, and ruthlessly exterminated his critics. Sima Qian (szoo-mah chee-en), the first-century B.C. author of China's earliest history, *Records of the Grand Historian,* called Qin Shi Huangdi "greedy and short-sighted. . . . He cast aside the kingly Way, . . . outlawing books and writings, making the laws and penalties much harsher, . . . leading the whole world in violence and cruelty."

After the First Emperor's death in 210 B.C., a rebel army rose up against Qin rule. The leader of the rebellion was Liu Bang (lyoo bong). This peasant warrior was a "kind and affectionate" man, wrote Sima Qian, with a "dragonlike face, . . . beautiful whiskers on his chin and cheeks [and] seventy-two black moles" (considered a lucky number). In 202 B.C. Liu Bang defeated the Qin forces. Declaring himself the new Son of Heaven, he founded the Han dynasty.

Han emperors ruled China for the next four hundred years. Later dynasties would look upon this period as a glorious age of strength and culture. The Han expanded the empire's borders through diplomacy and conquest. They opened up trade along the long route known as the Silk Road. They encouraged scholarship, science, technology, and the arts. In its might and glory, Han China equaled or surpassed the mighty Roman Empire, which flourished in the same era, far to the west.

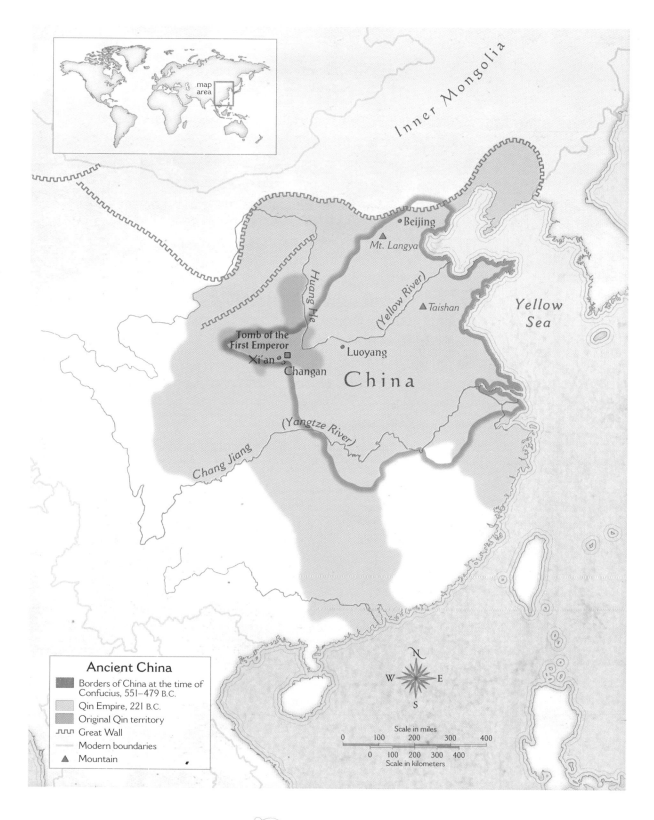

map area

Inner Mongolia

Beijing
▲ Mt. Langya

Huang He

(Yellow River)

▲ Taishan

Yellow Sea

Tomb of the
First Emperor

Xi'an

Changan

Luoyang

China

(Yangtze River)

Chang Jiang

Ancient China

- ▓ Borders of China at the time of Confucius, 551–479 B.C.
- ░ Qin Empire, 221 B.C.
- ▒ Original Qin territory
- ﻮﻮﻮ Great Wall
- —— Modern boundaries
- ▲ Mountain

N
W E
S

Scale in miles
0   100   200   300   400

0   100 200 300 400
Scale in kilometers

An Imperial Tour

After Qin Shi Huangdi united China in 221 B.C., he wanted to make sure everyone knew that he had the Mandate of Heaven. So the emperor began what we might call a public relations campaign. Traveling across his domain, he had inscriptions engraved on the mountaintops, praising his virtue and accomplishments. One of those tributes can still be read on northern China's Mount Langya:

> Great is the virtue of our Emperor
> Who pacifies all four corners of the earth, . . .
> All things flourish and grow;
> The common people know peace. . .
> Men delight in his rule,
> All understanding the law and discipline.
> The universe entire
> Is our Emperor's realm, . . .
> His kindness reaches even the beasts of the field;
> All creatures benefit from his virtue.

This painting from a later dynasty shows Qin Shi Huangdi touring his vast domain. The emperor unified China after more than two hundred years of civil war.

The glorious age of the Han ended in A.D. 220. To many historians, the dynasty's collapse marks the end of the ancient period of Chinese history.

Over the centuries that followed, dynasties rose and fell, but the traditions of imperial rule endured. Altogether, 157 emperors—from native-born heirs to Mongol conquerors—bore the awe-inspiring power and responsibility of Sons of Heaven.

Archaeologists discovered the tomb of Liu Sheng in Hebei province, northern China.

The Jade Prince

Historians first met Liu Sheng, son of the fourth Han emperor, Jingdi, in Sima Qian's *Records of the Grand Historian*. The prince "loved to drink and was very fond of women," wrote the ancient chronicler. He "pass[ed] his days listening to music and delighting himself with beautiful sights and sounds."

In 1968 archaeologists discovered Liu Sheng himself, buried deep inside a cliff in northern China. His tomb was designed like a palace, with stables, storerooms, kitchens, private apartments, and bathrooms. Its treasures offered evidence of the luxurious life at court. There were wine vessels, lamps, mirrors, incense burners, and ceremonial swords of bronze, silver, and gold.

Most precious of all was the prince's burial suit, made of 2,498 jade plaques sewn together with gold thread. Historians estimate that it would have taken ten years to make this elaborate body covering.

Liu Sheng was buried in a jade suit much like this one. The ancient Chinese believed that jade had magical properties that would preserve the body and guard against evil spirits.

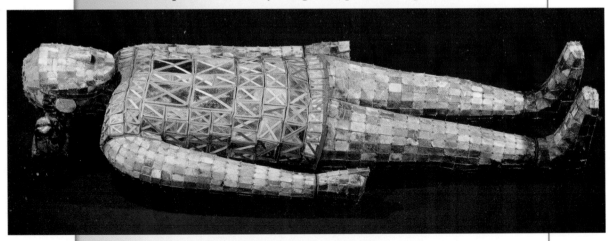

Chapter II

CIVIL SERVANTS AND NOBLES

The emperors were the supreme leaders of China's government. The day-to-day tasks of running the country, however, were carried out by thousands of officials. Government officials, or civil servants, were arranged in ranks in a highly organized **bureaucracy**.

Many of the highest-ranking civil servants lived and worked in the imperial capital. They advised the emperor and ran the main government departments. These included the ministries of war, justice, finance, public works, and religious rites.

Outside the capital China was divided into provinces. The provinces were further divided into smaller and smaller areas, from states and counties all the way down to local units of fifty to one hundred families. At each level of this multilayered

The Lost Capital

The first Han dynasty capital was Changan, in central China. At its height Changan was one of the largest and most splendid cities in the world. Hundreds of thousands of people lived within its protective walls, which stretched for 15 miles (24 kilometers) around the city.

Around A.D. 25, rebel forces destroyed Changan. After that, the Han moved their capital east, to Luoyang. In the seventh century the emperors of the Tang dynasty rebuilt Changan, but it fell again at their reign's end. Today the modern city of Xi'an (shee-on) sits atop the ruins of the ancient imperial capital.

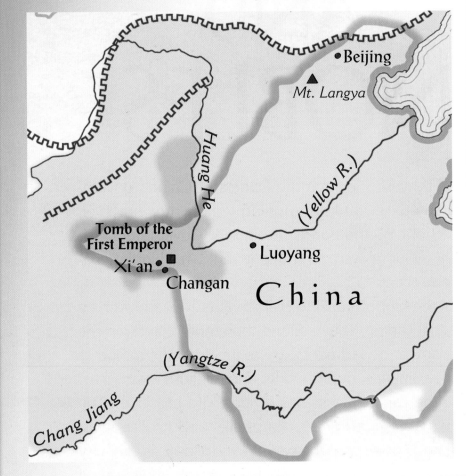

administrative system, civil servants enforced the laws and policies of the central government. They collected taxes, punished criminals, supervised building programs, raised troops, and kept registers of households and property.

The civil service was the most honored profession in ancient China. The higher an official's rank, the greater his wealth and social status. Rank was indicated by the color of his robes, the style of his headdress and carriage, even the number of courses served at his table. A government decree in 144 B.C. forbid other wealthy people from copying these signs of privilege. "Officials are the leaders of the populace," declared the order, "and it is right and proper that the carriages they ride in and the robes that they wear should correspond to the degree of their dignity."

Training for the Top

"Exceptional work demands exceptional men," read a proclamation by the fifth Han emperor, Wudi. "We therefore command the various district officials to search for men of brilliant and exceptional talents."

The civil service offered talented men from all levels of society a chance to rise to the ruling class. China's emperors believed that government rank should be based on ability, not on wealth or noble birth. Beginning in 196 B.C., senior officials throughout the empire were required to select a few young men each year who had demonstrated intelligence and high moral standards. These prospects were sent to the capital, where they were considered for government posts.

By later imperial times, the process of selecting officials had evolved into an ordeal that only the smartest and toughest could endure. Young men hoping to join the civil service spent years studying classic texts on history, government, and morality. Then they took a series of examinations. These exams might include a qualifying test in their local county, another in their provincial capital, and a "final exam" in the imperial capital.

Students taking the provincial exams were confined for nearly a week in tiny cells watched over by armed guards. Using brush

A Woman's Role

Only men could join the civil service. The women of ancient China were considered inferior to men and were expected to be submissive. According to the second-century A.D. advice book, *Admonitions of the Instructress to the Court Ladies,* "a female's proper role" was "humble, yielding, respectful and reverential."

Despite these restrictions, many upper-class women managed to gain considerable power, especially at the imperial court. Court ladies included the wives and concubines of the emperor and his top officials. Through clever advice and behind-the-scenes maneuvering, these women influenced important decisions, including the choice of the emperor's heir. Occasionally a woman might rule as **regent** for a young son. In the seventh century A.D., one determined woman, Wu Zetian, became a "Son of Heaven" in her own right.

and ink, they wrote out long answers to difficult essay questions. Their writing had to be perfect. No cross-outs or corrections were allowed. The penalties for cheating were severe. One emperor who learned of cheating in the imperial exam had the students disqualified and the examiners beheaded.

Only a tiny minority of students passed all their exams and joined the ranks of candidates qualified for civil service appointments. "The drudgery of yesterday is forgotten," wrote one lucky eighth-century graduate. "Today the prospects are vast, and my heart is filled with joy!"

Lifestyles of the Rich and Powerful

Like government officials, the nobles of ancient China were a privileged class. Nobles included relatives of the emperor and members of other important families. They were ranked by title, which they either inherited or received from the emperor as a reward for outstanding service.

High-ranking nobles and government officials lived in great luxury. Much of our knowledge of their lavish lifestyle comes from their tombs.

Archaeologists exploring Han tombs have found a treasure-house of precious objects crafted from jade, bronze, and lacquer (a hard, glossy material made from tree sap). Han tombs also held clay models of the homes and belongings of the wealthy. These elaborate miniatures include houses, pavilions, watchtowers, and farm buildings. They are complete to the smallest detail: fish cooking on the stove, tiny tables set with cups and chopsticks, watchdogs at the gate, birds on the roof.

Also specially made for the tomb were clay or wooden figures of servants. The burial chamber of one Han noblewoman contained 162 statuettes, some dressed in fine silk. These pint-size

Clay figures were often buried in the tombs of noblewomen. This type of statue shows us what the servants of wealthy nobles might have looked like.

figures were stand-ins for the lady's real-life attendants. In earlier ages living servants would have been sacrificed to serve her in the afterworld.

The Rewards of Rank

Images of the privileged life of the Han upper classes were carved or painted on tomb walls. More than fifty wall paintings decorated the six-room burial chamber of a civil servant who died in Inner Mongolia, northern China, around A.D. 170. The murals traced his career from his first appointment as a minor provincial official through his rise to the exalted rank of colonel-protector.

Like other high-ranking officials, the colonel owned magnificent homes in both the city and the countryside. The tomb murals show that his multistoried town house was graced with courtyards and gardens. His country estate was a complex of many buildings, all surrounded by walls and guarded by a tall watchtower.

The colonel drove elegant carriages and kept a stable of fine horses. Peasant farmers worked his fields and tended his cattle, sheep, and other livestock. In several of the paintings, his large body of servants are hard at work. These lower-class men and women kept his house and waited on his guests.

One of the murals shows a party of well-dressed visitors enjoying a lavish banquet. In ancient China the wealthy

At banquets upper-class men and women dined on a variety of fine dishes, while musicians, jugglers, and dancers provided entertainment. This illustration, which was impressed onto a brick, is from the Han dynasty.

A Noblewoman's Tomb

The tomb of Lady Xin, wife of the **marquis** of Dai, was packed with evidence of the luxurious lifestyle enjoyed by upper-class men and women in ancient China. The Han noblewoman died around 168 B.C. Her family stocked her burial chamber with a fortune in fine lacquer housewares and silk. Pots and baskets held all the ingredients for many splendid feasts. Recipes were jotted down on bamboo slips for the wooden servants that were placed nearby.

Lady Xin's tomb was so tightly sealed that her body was almost perfectly preserved. Archaeologists have used X-rays and other modern medical tools to examine her remains. Their diagnosis: The lady was about fifty years old, overweight, and out of shape. She died of a heart attack. She must have just eaten a hearty meal, because the scientists found 138 melon seeds still in her stomach.

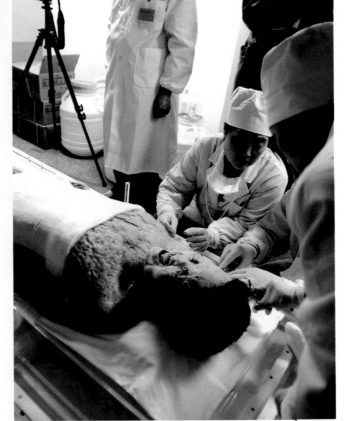

Archaeologists and medical personnel examine the body of Lady Xin.

dined on a wide variety of fruits and vegetables, as well as fish, pheasant, quail, turtle, pork, dog and horse meat, and sometimes exotic treats such as tiger meat and bear's paws. Dishes were seasoned with herbs and spices, combined in a "harmony of flavors." Men and women usually ate separately. In the mural the guests relaxing around the colonel's table probably include high-ranking officials and noblemen. A colorful company of musicians, dancers, and jugglers entertains them as they feast.

Chapter III

PHILOSOPHERS AND HOLY MEN

Ancient China's spirit world was home to a multitude of divine beings. Most important were the gods of nature. Nature spirits were everywhere—in the mountains, rivers, fields, forests, stars, wind, and thunder. They controlled everything from sickness and health to drought and rainfall to defeat and victory in battle. Heaven also included many ghostly ancestors. The ancestor spirits of former kings and emperors were especially wise and had mysterious godlike powers.

China's rulers were responsible for communicating with all these spirits. To help them with that important task, they surrounded themselves with priests, diviners, and shamans.

In Touch with the Spirits

In ancient China priests were government officials. Their work was considered so vital to the empire's well-being that it was supervised by a special department, the Ministry of Rites. Priests were in charge of performing the rituals that honored the spirits. They also built and maintained shrines at holy sites.

This painting found in the tomb of a noblewoman shows the spirits of the heavens and the underworld.

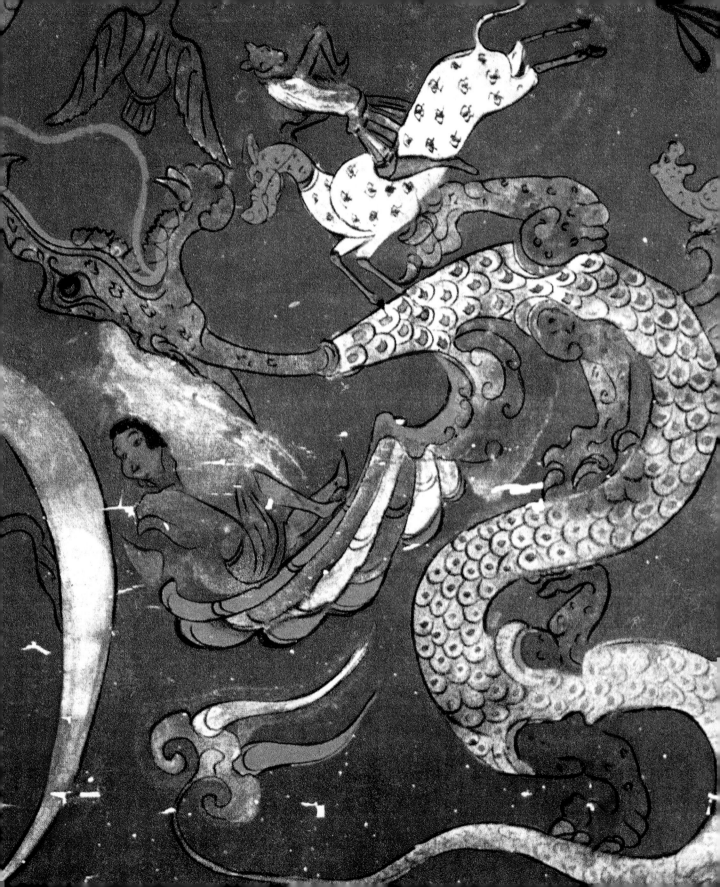

Diviners interpreted the signs of heaven's intentions. The appearance of a white peacock was a sure sign that the gods approved of a ruler. A rusty old sword, on the other hand, could be a bad omen. The gods might have placed the weapon in the soil for a rebel who would rise up and claim the Mandate of Heaven.

Shamans communicated directly with heaven. In prehistoric times these holy men and women were responsible for bringing rain. Entering a trance, the shaman was possessed by a spirit, which visited the world of mortals to share its gifts. In the days of the emperors, shamans were considered somewhat "primitive." They were generally consulted only in emergencies such as severe droughts or floods.

The Teachings of Confucius

During the closing centuries of the Zhou dynasty, before the empire was united, society was plagued by crime, corruption, and poverty. In those troubled times scholars traveled across China, seeking work in the courts of the kings. The most important of these wandering wise men was Kong Fuzi, known in the West as Confucius.

Born in 551 B.C., Confucius worked in several different states as a minor court official and teacher. In his lifetime he was not widely known. After his death, however, his students preserved and passed on the ideas he had developed in response to his chaotic times. Over the centuries Confucius came to be regarded as a divine being. His philosophy, known as Confucianism, had a deep and lasting influence on Chinese government and society.

Confucius taught that a people's well-being depended on order and morality. Everyone had a proper place in society, as well as duties to those higher and lower in the social scale. A good ruler honored the spirits. He also showed kindness and mercy to

Confucius is often considered the greatest philosopher of ancient China.

his subjects. In return, subjects should respect and obey their superiors and treat their inferiors justly. The *Analects,* a collection of Confucius's sayings compiled by his disciples, sums up that "golden rule" this way: "Do not do unto others what you would not have them do unto you."

Imperial China's highly structured government was based on Confucianism. So were relationships within the family, the basic building block of a happy and harmonious society. All members of a family were meant to love and respect one another, and proper sons and daughters showed respectful attention to the family elders. Other elements of Confucius's teachings that helped shape ancient Chinese society included his emphasis on proper performance of religious rituals and his respect for book learning.

In 124 B.C. Han emperor Wudi founded an imperial university where young men could study the *Analects* and other Confucian writings. Eventually, civil service candidates were expected to memorize more than 425,000 words from classic Confucian texts.

The Wisdom of the Way

Around the same time that Confucius was teaching, other philosophers were developing the basic ideas of Daoism (dow-ism). According to tradition, the father of Daoism was Laozi (low-zuh), a wise man who recorded his beliefs in the *Dao De Jing,* or "Way and Power Classic." However, historians aren't sure exactly when Laozi lived, and most believe that the classic Dao text was actually a collection of sayings by several philosophers.

After death the spirits of emperors and other wise men joined the gods and goddesses. This painting shows Laozi, the founder of Daoism, in the spirit world.

Daoists rejected the Confucian emphasis on the family as a model for good government. They believed that the answers to society's problems could be found only in nature. To achieve true happiness, people must turn their backs on ambition, wealth, and power. They must live a simple life, in tune with the natural rhythms of day and night, spring and winter, life and death. Only in this manner could they truly grasp the *Dao,* or "Way," that was the mystic source of all life and order in the universe.

Over the centuries Daoism took many forms. Some followers withdrew from society to live as hermits. Others used special diets, yogalike exercises, and "magic potions" in attempts to

The Dao De Jing

Daoism's classic text has been translated into more languages than any other book except the Bible. In the following passage the *Dao De Jing* urges readers to cease their pointless strivings for wealth and accomplishment.

> If you would not spill the wine,
> Do not fill the glass too full.
> If you wish your blade to hold its edge,
> Do not try to make it over-keen.
> If you do not want your house to be molested by robbers,
> Do not fill it with gold and jade.
> Wealth, rank, and arrogance add up to ruin,
> As surely as two and two are four.
> When you have done your work and established your fame,
>   withdraw!
> Such is the Way of Heaven.

achieve eternal life. Writers and painters were especially attracted to Daoism. In the philosophy's rejection of social restrictions and its closeness to nature, they found inspiration for some of China's most creative poetry and art.

The Buddhist Path to Bliss

Buddhism came to China from India in the first century A.D. through travelers along the Silk Road. At first most Chinese were suspicious of the foreign faith. Toward the end of the second century, however, in the upheavals that followed the fall of the Han dynasty, Buddhism began to take root.

The teachings of Buddhism offered comfort in difficult times. The faith's founder, an Indian prince known as the Buddha, or "Enlightened One," had taught that all unhappiness was caused by desire. Desire could be eliminated by following the Eightfold Noble Path: right understanding, right thought, right speech, right action, right livelihood, right moral effort, right mindfulness, and right concentration. The path would take followers to a state of **enlightenment** and endless bliss called nirvana.

Many Chinese practiced Buddhism alongside their more traditional faiths and philosophies. At work a civil servant might be a model of Confucian practices. Through rituals at home and at shrines, he would honor the nature gods and ancestor spirits. He might also try to lead a good life by following Buddhism's moral principles and guidance. At the end of a long day, he could surround himself with the beauties of nature, finding peace of mind in the mystical Way. A common saying reflected this unique blending of the faiths of Buddhism, Confucianism, and Daoism: "The three ways flow into one."

The Holiest Mountain

Spectacular evidence of China's unique blending of faiths lines the slopes of Taishan. This 5,000-foot (1,524-meter) mountain in eastern China has long been revered as a symbol of heaven. Qin Shi Huangdi climbed Taishan in 219 B.C., leaving behind an engraved stone slab proclaiming his virtues. Later emperors offered sacrifices and prayers at the peak of China's holiest mountain.

Today visitors to Taishan can stand in the spot where Confucius looked down on his homeland. They can trace the history of Daoism and Buddhism in the mountain's many shrines and temples. As they climb to the peak, they pass thousands of inscriptions by ancient emperors and philosophers. These include portions of classic Buddhist texts carved in Chinese **characters** nearly twice as tall as this page.

The slopes of Taishan are lined with carved inscriptions, temples, altars, pavilions, and other historical treasures.

PEASANT FARMERS AND SOLDIERS

Historians sometimes describe ancient China's society as a pyramid. At the top stood the emperor. Beneath him were the nobles and government officials. Below this privileged minority were the *shuren* ("people"), the great mass of subjects that included peasants, craft workers, and merchants. In the days of the Han dynasty, about two-thirds of China's people were peasant farmers.

Peasants were the backbone of society. Their work provided the food on which the entire empire depended. In Han times several imperial decrees recognized the peasant farmer's honorable status. An order from 141 B.C. opened with these lines: "Agriculture is the foundation of the empire. As for gold, pearls, and jade, they cannot be eaten in time of hunger, and cannot be worn in time of cold."

Despite their high official status, peasants were the most downtrodden members of society. Chao Cuo, an adviser to Han emperor Wendi, reflected on this contradiction. "The merchants,

This ancient stone carving shows peasants fishing in one of China's many waterways.

A Report to the Emperor

China's peasants were not buried with treasures. Their lives were rarely considered worthy subjects for poets and historians. To discover how peasant farmers lived, archaeologists often turn to government documents such as this second-century B.C. report by counselor Chao Cuo.

In spring they are exposed to the biting wind and dust; in summer they are subjected to the burning sun; numbed by the autumn rains, they shiver in winter. They have not a single day of rest in the whole year. . . . They are harassed by a thousand chores, and further overwhelmed by natural disasters [and] unseasonable collection of taxes. . . . The peasant is often obliged to sell all his property, his fields, his house and sometimes even his children and grandchildren to settle his debts.

whom laws and regulations disparage [disapprove], are rich and honored," he wrote, "while the peasantry, which the same laws honor, is poor and despised."

Old Ways and New

In northern China there is little rainfall and the winters are bitter cold. Farmers there grew mainly wheat and **millet**. In the warmer, wetter south, rice became the main crop. Many farmers also grew vegetables and fruits, including beans, gourds, snow peas, strawberries, dates, and melons. Hemp plants provided the fibers that were woven into the coarse cloth used for peasants' clothes.

Most of these crops were grown on small independent farms. In early imperial times peasant farmers still used many of the same simple tools as their ancestors. They tilled the soil with wooden plows and stone hoes. They harvested grain with stone knives and scythes. To separate the grain from the harvested crops, they beat the plants with wooden tools called flails.

Around the beginning of the Han dynasty, a few new tools made the peasant farmer's work a little easier and more productive. The most important innovation was the iron plow. Iron plowshares (the tips of the plows) did not break as easily as wood, and they cut deeper furrows. Some farmers equipped their new plows with moldboards. These laborsaving devices pushed the dirt aside so that it would not pile up in front of the plow.

The Han era also saw the development of better irrigation systems. These were especially useful in the cultivation of rice, which is grown in flooded fields. The "endless chain," a machine invented around A.D. 100, pumped water from streams and

Peasants water their crops using an endless chain irrigation pump.

決水復沈弘
農候生用莊
桔橰取諸井

irrigation ditches to farm fields. The pump was operated by foot power. Two men working the pedals could water the fields for an entire village.

A Family Affair

The whole family worked together to run a peasant farm. An old Chinese saying described the division of labor: "Man as tiller, woman as weaver." While the head of the household worked the soil, his wife made the family's clothes: tunics and trousers from hemp, hats and rain capes from rice straw, sandals from hemp or straw. She prepared their simple meals of grain, fruit, vegetables, and sometimes a bit of chicken or fish. She gathered herbs and made the family's medicines. Some women raised silkworms. The threads from the cocoons could be spun and woven into silk cloth, which was sold to raise extra cash. Women also pitched in when extra hands were needed in the fields.

Children worked alongside their parents. Even very young children had chores such as taking care of the livestock. Farm animals usually included a few chickens, ducks, pigs, or sheep. Fortunate families owned oxen to pull the plow.

The farm household also might include the farmer's parents. They did their share of the work and were treated with the respect due to elders. All the members of the family lived together in a small, crowded wooden hut.

At special times throughout the year, the peasant family took time to honor the spirits. The most important religious observance was the New Year's festival. On this solemn occasion families offered gifts of food and wine to the god of the hearth. They raised their cups to the spirits of their ancestors. In prayers they asked for protection from the many hardships plaguing the life of the peasant farmer.

The Peasants' Burdens

Farm families lived at the mercy of nature. A flood or drought could destroy an entire year's harvest. Faced with starvation, the peasant farmer might have to sell his few possessions, including the tools and livestock needed to run the farm. He might even be forced to sell his own children into slavery.

To buy seeds for the next year's crops, a poor farmer could borrow money from a wealthy landowner. If he was unable to repay his debts, he lost his land. Some landless peasants became servants in well-to-do households. Most went to work as tenant farmers, tending a landlord's fields and paying rent that could equal half or more of their produce.

Adding to the peasants' burdens were their government obligations. In good years and bad, farmers had to pay taxes, usually in grain. Able-bodied men also were required to work for one month a year in the government's labor force. They might be assigned to iron or salt mines or to one of the many imperial building projects. Honest peasants worked alongside convict laborers building palaces, tombs, roads, canals, and defensive walls. Conditions were harsh, and many laborers died from cold, hunger, and exhaustion.

In 1972 a team of Chinese archaeologists uncovered the graves of some ten thousand workers who had died while building the tomb of Han emperor Jingdi. Engraved bricks identified the dead. Some were convicted criminals, with iron shackles still clamped around their necks or ankles. Others were peasants who had been drafted for public works projects.

The Terra-cotta Warriors

The peasant farmer was also a soldier. All able-bodied men of the lower classes were required to serve in the army, usually for a

period of two years. Most peasants became infantrymen, or foot soldiers. In peacetime they might serve as couriers carrying official mail or guards manning the watchtowers along the empire's frontiers. Soldiers were also put to work alongside the laborers on government building projects.

In times of rebellion, invasion, and campaigns of conquest, soldiers were sent into battle. Much of what we know about the early imperial armies comes from official government reports and scenes in paintings and sculpture. By far the richest source of information are Emperor Qin Shi Huangdi's **terra-cotta** warriors.

In 1974 farmers digging a well near Xi'an, in central China, discovered broken bits of statues in the soil. Archaeologists were called in to investigate. Over the following months they unearthed one of the most remarkable finds in history. More than six thousand life-size terra-cotta soldiers and horses waited beneath the ground. This vast underground army had been buried in huge pits near the tomb of the First Emperor at his death in 210 B.C. to protect him for all eternity.

The clay soldiers stand in battle formation, ready to fight. Leading the army are the archers, each holding a powerful **cross-bow**. Behind the archers, horses pull the remains of wooden chariots. Next come row after row of infantrymen. These common soldiers wear lightly armored vests and carry real bronze lances, spears, knives, and axes. Protecting the sides and rear of the formation are cavalrymen on horseback.

By studying Qin Shi Huangdi's buried warriors, archaeologists have learned a great deal about ancient uniforms, armor, and equipment. The arrangement of the troops has revealed some secrets of ancient Chinese military strategy. Even the faces of the soldiers tell a story. Each of the carefully crafted figures has its own

The First Emperor's tomb was one of the greatest archaeological discoveries of the twentieth century. No two soldiers in this vast terra-cotta army look exactly alike.

unique personality. Older officers with calm, thoughtful expressions lead young men who seem proud, nervous, or excited. Many of the soldiers look bone-tired. Perhaps they are reflecting on the words of an ancient Chinese folk song:

Long ago, when we started, the willows spread their shade.
Now that we turn back the snowflakes fly.
The march before us is long, we are thirsty and hungry.
Our hearts are stricken with sorrow,
but no one listens to our plaint.

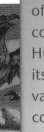

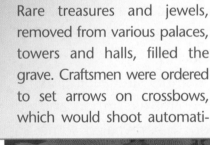

The First Emperor's Tomb

The terra-cotta warriors are part of a gigantic underground complex centered on Qin Shi Huangdi's tomb. The tomb itself has not yet been excavated. For a description of its contents, we turn to ancient historian Sima Qian.

Rare treasures and jewels, removed from various palaces, towers and halls, filled the grave. Craftsmen were ordered to set arrows on crossbows, which would shoot automatically at anyone breaking in. Rivers and seas in miniature were dug and filled with mercury, made to flow by mechanical devices. On the ceiling, stars and planets were set, on the floor **topographical** features of the earth. . . . When the funeral was finished, . . . all those who had been employed as workers or artisans for hiding the treasures were shut inside; they could not get out.

Chapter V

ARTISANS AND SILK MAKERS

The third level in ancient Chinese society, after the government officials and peasant farmers, was made up of artisans, or craftspeople. Artisans were considered productive members of society. They made practical goods such as tools, weapons, housewares, harnesses, and carriages. They also turned out luxury items, including fine jewelry and elaborately patterned silk.

Artisans worked at both government-run factories and private workshops. Most of the goods they produced were commonplace items that even a farm family could afford. Chinese craft workers, however, often brought a skill and artistry to their work that transformed everyday objects into works of art.

The Potter's Craft

From very early times the Chinese made pottery that was both useful and decorative. Many of the clay vessels found at prehistoric sites were covered with painted designs, from swirling

Chinese craft workers produced the goods needed for daily life, such as tools, as well as objects of great beauty, such as jewelry.

lines to images of fanciful demons. One four-thousand-year-old jug was shaped like a pig, with an open mouth for a spout.

At first Chinese potters shaped their vessels by hand. Sometime around 3000 B.C. they learned how to use a potter's wheel. By imperial times, pottery making had become a sophisticated art.

The artisans who made Qin Shi Huangdi's terra-cotta warriors worked on an "assembly line." Archaeologists have figured out the techniques they used from clues they left behind, such as fingerprints in the clay. From inscriptions on the statues, they know that at least eighty-five master craftsmen worked on the challeng-

ing project. Each had a team of ten to twelve assistants. These less skilled workers were assigned to different steps in the production process. Some mixed clay. Some coiled long strips of clay to form the soldiers' bodies. Some workers used molds to make the hands, ears, beards, and other small parts, while others fastened the parts together.

The master added the fine details that gave each figure its unique personality. He also painted the finished soldiers in bright colors. Although the paint did not survive the long centuries underground, scientists have been able to re-create it from chemical traces left on the statues.

This is the back of a bronze mirror made during the Qin dynasty. The ancient Chinese believed that mirrors had magical powers.

Beautiful Bronzes

Chinese metalworkers made sturdy farm tools and weapons from iron. They shaped silver and gold into priceless hairpins, necklaces, earrings, and belt buckles. Some of their most beautiful and intricate treasures were made from bronze.

The Chinese discovered how to combine copper and tin to make bronze about four thousand years ago. During the Shang dynasty, metalworkers crafted exquisite bronze containers for the food and wine offered in religious rituals. Shang vessels were often elaborately decorated with intertwining images of real and mythical creatures, such as birds, tigers, elephants, and dragons.

In Han times artisans working in government factories made bronze weapons and coins. Private workshops supplied wealthy buyers with bronze housewares and luxury goods, including wine vessels, incense burners, vases, and sculpture.

Bronze mirrors were especially popular. Polished to a reflective glow on one side and decorated with sacred symbols on the other, they were believed to have magical properties. One mirror crafted around A.D. 100 carried this inscription: "The *shangfang* workshop has made this mirror to keep all misfortunes away; . . . The dragon on the left and the tiger on the right keep harmful

Metalworking Methods

China's earliest bronze objects were made in clay molds. Hot liquid bronze was poured into the space between a center mold and an outer mold. After the bronze cooled and hardened, workers removed the molds and later reused them.

Around 500 B.C. the Chinese also began making bronzes with the "lost-wax" method. First, workers made a wax model of an object, which they carved with fine designs. They covered the model inside and out with clay to make a mold. When they heated the mold, the wax melted and flowed away. Then hot bronze was poured into the space where the wax had been. After the metal cooled, the artisans broke the mold. Bronzes made with the lost-wax method were highly detailed, one-of-a-kind treasures.

influences away; . . . May you long keep your two parents and know joy, wealth, and prosperity."

Treasures from Sap

The ancient Chinese were the first to use lacquer. Craft workers started with the sticky sap of an east Asian lacquer tree. Heated and purified, the sap became a thin gray liquid, which could be colored with powdered minerals.

Liquid lacquer was painted in very thin layers on a base of wood, bamboo, cloth, or metal. A fine vessel might receive as many as two hundred coats. Each took several days to dry. Dozens of different artisans had a hand in coating the object, carving or painting it with delicate designs, adding gold or silver decorations, and polishing it to a glow.

Lacquerware was highly prized in ancient China. This beautiful vessel was used for serving food.

All that time and labor was reflected in the finished product's price. A fine lacquered bowl could cost ten times as much as one made from bronze. Regardless of its expense, lacquerware was extremely popular with officials and nobles, who admired both its beauty and its durability.

Lacquerware's hard finish was remarkably resistant to heat, acid, and water. The archaeologists who excavated Lady Xin's tomb found dozens of lacquered objects, including dishes, vases, armrests, cosmetic boxes, and the noblewoman's three nested coffins. These two-thousand-year-old treasures were all as smooth and lustrous as the day they were buried.

Secrets of Silk

The ancient Chinese were also the first to make silk. Sometime during the Shang dynasty, they discovered that a certain caterpillar's cocoon could be transformed into strong, smooth, shimmering cloth.

Silk comes from silkworms. Silk makers raised silkworm caterpillars in special temperature-controlled rooms, feeding them on the leaves of mulberry trees. The caterpillars spun a thick cocoon from a single filament (very fine thread) of pale yellow silk. Before the cocoons could hatch into moths, some were dropped into boiling water. That killed the worms and softened the silk. The silk makers unraveled the filaments, cleaned them, and spun them together to make a strong thread. Then the thread was dyed and woven into cloth.

In imperial times silk making was a big business. Government-run factories, private workshops, and small home operations turned out silk cloth in many different colors, patterns, and textures. The prized fabric was worn by emperors, nobles, and wealthy officials. It was also traded along the Silk Road as far west as Rome. Each bale of silk was worth its weight in gold.

The Chinese kept the techniques used in producing their most valuable export a closely guarded secret for centuries. The penalty for revealing the silk maker's secrets to a foreigner was death.

Silk Blessings

None of the looms used for weaving silk in early imperial times has survived. However, archaeologists have found sketches of Han dynasty looms more sophisticated than anything that would be seen in the West for another four hundred years. They have also unearthed many samples of silk cloth. These include fabrics bearing good-luck wishes. Chinese artisans "programmed" their looms with punched cards to print these messages in the pattern of the cloth as it was woven. A nobleman's robes might carry prayers for "ten thousand lifetimes and all you wish" or "many years and long life, with a goodly blessing of sons and grandsons."

This is a replica of a loom used during the Han dynasty.

MERCHANTS AND TRADERS

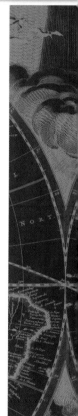

Merchants took last place in ancient Chinese society. Unlike farmers and artisans, they did not produce anything useful. Instead, they bought and sold the things that other people made. That was considered dishonorable. One merchant wrote in a letter to a friend that he was ashamed by his "vile and humiliating position. . . . One who is a man of low standing, where all defamations [accusations] will flow in upon him, is trembling without being cold."

Despite their low status, successful merchants gained considerable wealth and influence. They built mansions on huge estates. Their sons became civil servants, and their daughters married nobles. Merchants "neither plow nor weed," complained one Han statesman, "[but they] ride in well-built cars and whip up fat horses, wear shoes of silk and trail white silk behind them."

In the Marketplace

Every Chinese town had at least one market. Large cities such as Changan had several. Markets were busy, noisy, crowded places where people of all ranks gathered to buy and sell, eat and drink, entertain and be entertained.

61

This stone carving shows a typical market scene during the Han dynasty.

Shops and stalls were laid out in rows in the marketplace. Merchants selling the same types of goods were grouped together. There were specialists in fruits and vegetables, pots and pans, sheep, pigs, and chickens. Hardware shops offered iron and brass equipment. Drapers carried coarse hemp cloth and fine silk. Peddlers sold hot and cold snacks, while better restaurants served up fine wine and delicacies. Diviners told fortunes. Strolling jugglers and acrobats performed. Meanwhile, government officials kept an eye on every transaction, making sure that no one sold prohibited goods such as out-of-season game and that shopkeepers paid their market taxes.

Beginning in Qin times, shoppers paid for their purchases with small round copper coins known as "cash." The coins had a square hole in the center and were strung together on cords. An oxcart might sell for 2,000 cash. An adult female slave could cost 20,000.

Slaves included poor people who had been sold to pay their debts, criminals enslaved for their crimes, and prisoners of war. They performed a variety of jobs: bodyguard, laborer, clerk, messenger, servant, musician, dancer. Native-born slaves were sometimes freed by their owners in reward for faithful service. From time to time all slaves were set free by government decree.

The fishmonger's stall was a common sight in China's lively marketplaces. This merchant may have brought his goods to market on a small wooden sampan.

By Land and Water

Merchants took their goods to market along China's roads and waterways. Under Qin Shi Huangdi laborers built a network of wide earthen roads connecting all parts of the empire. However, these imperial highways were for the exclusive use of the emperor and his messengers and officials. Merchants and other less privileged members of society had to use narrow foot-worn tracks.

It was often easier to travel by water. China has several long rivers, which run from west to east. Beginning in the fifth century B.C., canals were built to connect the rivers and carry goods and people north and south. Han emperor Wudi built a canal 80 miles (130 kilometers) long, linking Changan with the Yellow River. Seven centuries later, emperors of the Sui dynasty built the Grand Canal between the Yellow and Yangtze Rivers, connecting northern and southern China.

Clay models found in Han tombs show the kinds of boats used on China's waterways. The most common craft were sampans. These small flat-bottomed wooden boats were propelled by short oars. Bamboo canopies or huts offered protection for products and passengers.

Along the Silk Road

For centuries China's only foreign contacts were with the **nomadic** peoples who lived to the north and frequently raided the borderlands. Around 138 B.C. Han emperor Wudi sent out an expedition seeking allies to fight the nomads. His envoy Zhang Qian (jang chee-en) traveled west into the unknown lands of central Asia. He was captured by nomads, who held him prisoner for ten years. Finally he escaped and completed his journey. When Zhang Qian returned home, he brought surprising news: other rich civilizations existed outside the Middle Kingdom.

Before long, China's merchants had set up rich trade links with the lands to the west. Some goods traveled by sea. Most went by land, along the Silk Road.

The Silk Road wasn't really a road. It was an unpaved trail with several branches leading from Changan through central Asia, across Persia (modern-day Iran), to the eastern shores of the Mediterranean Sea. Along its 5,000-mile (8,000-kilometer) route, the Silk Road passed through some of the world's harshest regions. It climbed steep mountains along narrow passes. It crossed treacherous deserts that were blazing hot by day, bitter

The Silk Road linked China with the West. This photograph shows modern-day travelers exploring the ancient trade route.

cold at night. In northwestern China's Taklimakan Desert, sand dunes could drift as high as 300 feet (90 meters), swallowing up an entire village. Turkish traders gave this desert its name, which means "go in and you won't come out."

To travel these perilous paths, merchants banded together in a trade **caravan**. Caravans often included hundreds of people. Two-humped **Bactrian camels** carried the trade goods and supplies. These hardy animals could go long distances without water. According to an old Chinese chronicle, they also served as weather forecasters. When a sandstorm approached, the older camels would "stand snarling together, and bury their mouths in the sand. The men always take this as a sign, and they too immediately cover their noses and mouths by wrapping them in felt."

Caravans might travel from 10 to 50 miles (6.2 to 31 km) a day. From time to time they stopped to rest and resupply at one of the towns and trading centers that grew up alongside the Silk Road.

The entire journey from one end of the Silk Road to the other took many months. Few people ever traveled the whole way. Instead, each merchant carried his goods from one trading center to the next, then sold or exchanged them before returning home. Other merchants took the merchandise farther along the road.

Because transport was so difficult and expensive, only luxury goods were traded along the Silk Road. China's most valued export, of course, was silk. Chinese traders also carried pottery, bronze, lacquerware, spices, and squirrel or fox furs. In return they might bring back horses, wool, glass, pearls, and exotic animals such as lions and rhinoceroses.

Mostly, though, the Chinese traded silk for gold. The people of the Roman Empire were especially eager for the prized fabric. In fact, Rome's lavish spending on silk drained its gold supplies and weakened its economy, eventually contributing to the fall of the empire.

A City in the Sand

In 1900 a team of Swedish explorers stumbled across the ruins of a few wooden houses in the Taklimakan Desert. After a quick search the men headed back to camp. One returned to retrieve a shovel. He found that a sandstorm had blown through, exposing a large brick fortress. The explorers had discovered the ancient city of Loulan, buried for 1,500 years.

Loulan was a caravan stop on the Silk Road. During the Han dynasty, it became a large, prosperous community. Over time desert sands buried the city. They also protected its remains. Archaeologists have unearthed perfectly preserved sheepskin clothing, leather shoes, grass baskets, and letters written on wooden tablets. They have also found startlingly lifelike bodies, turned into mummies by the dry sands.

The ancient city of Loulan

Chapter VII

INVENTORS, SCIENTISTS, AND HEALERS

Many advances in science and technology traveled with the silk and other trade goods from China along the Silk Road. Westerners often had no idea of the origin of these marvels. In fact, a number of innovations once thought to have originated in Europe actually came from the ancient Chinese.

China's "firsts" included many practical objects developed to solve everyday problems. No one knows who was responsible for them or exactly when they appeared. Early innovations included the wheelbarrow, the crossbow, the iron plow, the magnetic compass, the ship's **rudder**, and the waterwheel, which used waterpower to run factory machines. Sometime in the fourth century B.C., the Chinese invented a new kind of harness for horses and other farm animals. The trace harness rested on the chest instead of the neck, allowing the animal to pull heavier loads without choking. This simple but important innovation would not appear in Europe for another nine hundred years.

One of the most important Chinese inventions was paper. The world's oldest piece of paper, discovered in a tomb in northern China in 1957, was made from pounded hemp fibers during the reign of Han emperor Wudi. Early paper was so thick and strong that it was frequently used for curtains, clothing, and even light armor.

The ancient Chinese are credited with many inventions, including the magnetic compass.

An Ingenious Machine

In A.D. 132 Han scientist Zhang Heng (jang hung) invented the first seismograph, or earthquake detector. This ingenious instrument could detect an earthquake occurring far from the imperial capital, allowing the emperor to rush aid to devastated areas.

Zhang Heng's seismograph was designed like a huge bronze jar, with a pendulum inside. Eight dragon heads ringed the jar. Metal toads stood in a circle beneath the dragons. When distant tremors shook the device, the pendulum swung. A ball was knocked out of the mouth of the dragon facing the origin of the quake, into the mouth of a toad. According to historical records, soon after Zhang Heng set up his device, it recorded an earthquake more than 300 miles (480 kilometers) west of the capital.

Scientists and Stargazers

Ancient China's scientists searched for divine messages in the skies and for magic potions granting eternal life. Today we might find the ideas behind their work peculiar. Their careful experiments and observations, however, led to discoveries that would influence scientific advances throughout the world for centuries.

China's most important science was astronomy. Ancient **astronomers** worked for the king or emperor, studying the sun, moon, and stars in order to predict celestial events. The Son of Heaven was supposed to rule in harmony with the universe. An unexpected comet or eclipse could be seen as evidence that he had lost the Mandate of Heaven.

Clues in the Night Sky

Ancient China's fascination with astronomy and astrology has provided a treasure trove of information to modern-day historians. In the 1980s American professor David Pankenier studied historical accounts written by imperial scholars. He found that the ancient chroniclers often paired their accounts of wars and natural disasters with observations of celestial events such as eclipses and comets, which they believed were signs of heaven's role in human affairs. Using computer models, the professor created pictures of the night sky at different times in the past. Then he compared those images with the observations in the ancient writings. His findings helped him pinpoint key dates in China's distant past, such as the year Zhou rebels overthrew the Shang dynasty. That year, 1046 B.C, may be the earliest precisely known date in human history.

Rulers were also served by **astrologers**. These advisers used the information gathered by astronomers to make predictions about human affairs such as battles. In ancient China the science of astronomy and the mystical practice of astrology were closely linked and equally respected.

Archaeologists have found records of eclipses of the sun and moon inscribed on Shang oracle bones. Chinese astronomers also kept the ancient world's most complete and accurate records of comets, meteors, **supernova** stars, and **sunspots**. They created the first scientific star map and invented the armillary sphere, the first instrument for measuring the position and movement of the planets.

Searching for the Great Elixir

Another important ancient science was alchemy. Chinese alchemists searched for a way to change common metals such as lead into gold, which would last forever. They believed that if they could find the right method, they would at the same time discover the **elixir** of life. This magical combination of substances would make mortal men immortal.

The best-known Chinese alchemist was Ko Hung. In the fourth century A.D., he wrote a book describing the ideal working conditions for seekers of the great elixir. He advised alchemists to set up isolated laboratories on sacred mountains. Before conducting their experiments, they should fast and anoint themselves with aromatic oils. Ko Hung's text included this formula for the elixir of life:

After cooking for thirty days, a mixture of Chin 1 [gold fluid] and quicksilver [mercury] is placed in a yellow earthen jar, which is then sealed with Six-One Mud and strongly heated for sixty hours. Thereupon the medicine is obtained. The swallowing of a pea-sized quantity of the medicine is enough to make a hsien [immortal] out of any person.

Some of the alchemists' potions for extending life actually had the opposite effect. Elixirs containing mercury and arsenic, for example, were deadly poisons. Several emperors, including Qin Shi Huangdi, probably died early deaths from elixir poisoning.

Although alchemists never achieved their goals, they did discover new compounds and make important observations of chemical reactions. The work of the alchemists of China and other ancient civilizations formed the basis of modern chemistry. In their experiments with minerals and plants, Chinese alchemists also discovered many healing drugs that are still valued today.

Healing Body and Spirit

The Chinese practice of medicine dates back more than four thousand years. By early imperial times, most healers were specialists. They might be veterinarians, researchers, or experts in treating sick or injured people.

Medicine was one of the few professions open to women. Midwives helped farm women during childbirth. Well-respected female doctors treated well-to-do women, including ladies of the imperial court.

A doctor treating a sick merchant or noble would perform a thorough exam, consult the patient's medical records, and write out a prescription. The Han-era tomb of Lady Xin's son contained medical texts with hundreds of prescriptions for curing various illnesses. These remedies included special diets and exercises, as well as medicines made from herbs and minerals.

Another common form of medical treatment was acupuncture. This practice was based on the idea that natural energy, or *qi,* flowed through the body along twelve invisible lines linked to different organs. Doctors performing acupuncture inserted fine needles in the patient's skin at specific points along the lines. This was believed to correct the flow of *qi* and heal the body.

Another important idea behind Chinese medicine was the concept of yin and yang. The ancient Chinese believed that everything in the world was made up of these two natural forces. The yin force was dark, cool, damp, and submissive. Yang was bright, warm, dry, and dominant. When the forces of yin and yang were unbalanced in the body, a person became sick. A healthful diet could correct the balance. So could restoring the proper flow of *qi* through acupuncture.

The basic medical text of Han China, the *Yellow Emperor's Classic of Medicine,* examined the importance of yin and yang:

> If Yang is overly powerful, then Yin may be too weak. If Yin is particularly strong, then Yang is apt to be defective. . . . Experts in examining patients judge their general appearance; they feel their pulse and determine whether it is Yin or Yang that causes the disease. . . . When one is filled with vigor and strength, Yin and Yang are in proper harmony.

Chapter VIII

WRITERS AND ARTISTS

China has one of the world's oldest written languages. The earliest-known Chinese writing appeared more than three thousand years ago, on the Shang oracle bones. Over time many different versions of writing developed across the far-flung lands of the Middle Kingdom. In the third century B.C., the First Emperor combined these various styles into one standard form. During the Han dynasty, government officials refined this written language so that they could express ideas more quickly and easily. With minor changes, the style of writing they developed is still used in China today.

Chinese is written in characters. Each of these symbols stands for a word or part of a word. Some characters represent simple objects, such as *fish* or *sun.* Some are formed by combining two or more characters. For example, *sun* and *moon* together make *bright.* Many characters for complex

ideas combine basic characters with category markers and other special symbols.

This flexible system of writing gave rise to a vast vocabulary for creating beautifully expressive literature. It was also extremely complicated. The first Chinese dictionary, compiled by Han scholars in A.D. 121, included more than 9,000 characters. That number eventually grew to more than 40,000. Each character had to be memorized separately. In ancient times few people besides the men of the upper classes had the time to learn how to read and write more than a few words in Chinese.

The Calligrapher's Art

Chinese characters are more than just the building blocks of an expressive language. They are also beautiful in themselves. Since the days of the Han scholars, calligraphy (the art of elegant handwriting) has been one of China's most important arts.

Calligraphers wrote with brushes made from soft animal hairs. They mixed their ink by grinding a solid ink stick into a few drops of water on an inkstone. Producing the right consistency of ink was part of the calligrapher's craft. According to one Chinese master, "Five colors can be obtained from black ink alone."

The calligrapher held his brush straight up, without resting his wrists or elbows on the table. He drew the characters with swift, fluid motions. Each character was formed from up to twenty-six brushstrokes, which had to be written in a precise order.

A calligrapher would use this inkstone or slab to mix the ink to the proper thickness.

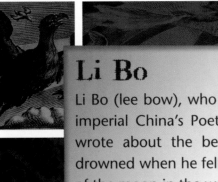

Li Bo

Li Bo (lee bow), who lived in the eighth century A.D., is known as imperial China's Poet Immortal. Inspired by Daoism, Li Bo often wrote about the beauties of nature. According to legend, he drowned when he fell from a boat trying to embrace the reflection of the moon in the water.

These verses are from Li Bo's poem "Alone Looking at the Mountain."

All the birds have flown up and gone;
A lonely cloud floats leisurely by.
We never tire of looking at each other—
Only the mountain and I.

Just as important as correct form was a character's *qi.* Like the energy flowing through the human body, *qi* gave the characters their "life." Artists practiced for years perfecting their brushwork in order to give their writing the qualities of life, energy, strength, and movement. One master calligrapher wrote that brushstrokes should be "like a flock of birds darting out of the forest, or like a frightened snake disappearing in the grass."

The Spirit of Painting

Painters worked with the same tools as calligraphers: brushes, inkstones, and ink. They too tried to capture not just the likeness of a subject but also its *qi.* Eighth-century A.D. painter Wang Wei described a painting with that mysterious quality:

While this painting was made in a later period, it reflects the landscape-painting style of tenth-century China. Nature elements such as mountains and water, dominate the image, which depicts a peach blossom spring.

The wind rises from the green forest, and the foaming water rushes in the stream. Alas! Such painting cannot be achieved by physical movements of the fingers and hand, but only by the spirit entering into them. This is the nature of painting.

Early Chinese artists painted animated scenes of country, city, and court life. They also painted real plants and animals and mythical beasts, especially dragons. In the seventh century A.D., brightly colored scenes from Buddhist texts became popular. In the tenth century, under the Song dynasty, the artists' interest shifted to landscape painting.

Landscapes were often painted in shades of black ink on long silk scrolls. These panoramic views of mountains, rivers, and waterfalls reflected nature's beauty and majesty. Artists used overlapping shapes as well as contrasts between towering peaks and smaller foothills to give a sense of changing height and depth. As the scroll was unrolled, the landscape was revealed. Almost like a modern motion picture, it drew the viewer's eyes into an ever-changing scene.

Poetry and the Three Perfections

China's earliest poems were songs. Sung or chanted to a musical accompaniment, they were often inspired by everyday concerns such as marriage, work, hunting, or war. Later poets wrote on a variety of themes, including nature, love, longing, wine, and the impermanence of life.

The following poem (which rhymes in the original Chinese) was written around 110 B.C. by Chinese princess Xijun (also called Hsi-chün), a daughter of Han emperor Wudi. Like many other wellborn young women, the princess was married to a man

A Buried Orchestra

China's arts included sacred music, played during religious rituals, and popular music, enjoyed by people at all levels of society. In 1978 archaeologists exploring a fourth-century B.C. tomb heard echoes of some of these long-ago tones.

Marquis Yi was a rich and powerful Zhou nobleman. Among the treasures buried in his tomb was an entire orchestra. There were flutes, panpipes, mouth organs, **zithers**, and drums. Sixty-four bronze bells, ranging from 8 inches (20 centimeters) to 5 feet (1.5 meters) tall, hung from a lacquered stand. When they were struck with wooden mallets, the bells played a symphony of liquid notes.

Archaeologists also found the remains of twenty-one young women buried near the instruments. These included several unfortunate musicians, sacrificed upon the nobleman's death to entertain him in the afterworld.

chosen by her parents for his wealth and political connections. Xijun's husband was a central Asian nomad. "The Lament of Hsi-chün" expresses her loneliness and longing for home.

> My people have married me
> In a far corner of Earth:
> Sent me away to a strange land,
> To the king of the Wu-sun.
> A tent is my house,
> Of felt are my walls;
> Raw flesh my food
> With mare's milk to drink.
> Always thinking of my own country,
> My heart sad within.
> Would I were a yellow stork
> And could fly to my old home!

During the Song dynasty, the arts of poetry, calligraphy, and painting became known as the "three perfections." Combining the three perfections in a single work was considered the highest form of expression. An artist might paint a landscape on silk, inspiring a poet to write a verse. The poem was then inscribed on the painting by a master calligrapher.

Sometimes the poem came first. Song emperor Huizong (hway zung) liked to hold competitions for his most talented government ministers. Assigning a line or two of verse, he challenged the officials to create a painting inspired by the poetic images. On one occasion the emperor presented this verse: "The horses' hooves were fragrant on returning from trampling flowers." The winning painting showed butterflies fluttering behind the hooves of galloping horses.

遺陵之禍腐刑慘酷
發憤成書良史實錄

司馬遷

The works of Sima Qian have provided a great deal of information about the history of ancient China.

The Dangerous Lives of Historians

To modern readers, early China's history books sometimes seem more like novels. Ancient Chinese writers presented history as a series of exciting episodes in the lives of famous people. They often made up speeches and conversations to let their characters tell their own tales. Their chronicles always included a moral regarding proper behavior or the dangers of misrule.

China's first historian, Sima Qian, had an ambitious goal: telling the whole of human history. To him, that meant the story

An Educated Woman

While Chinese boys studied philosophy, government, and the arts, their sisters learned how to care for a family and make offerings to the spirits. A few young women of the upper classes, however, enjoyed greater opportunities.

Ban Zhao was the daughter of a Han scholar who gave his sons and daughters the same excellent education. In her *Lessons for Women,* a guide to proper feminine behavior, she echoed the Confucian belief that a woman should "put others first, herself last." At the same time Ban Zhao argued that girls should receive "a literary education as well as . . . training in good manners" so that they might become "correct in manner and upright in character."

of the Middle Kingdom from the distant days of legendary god-kings to his own lifetime in the reign of Han emperor Wudi.

While Sima Qian was writing his *Records of the Grand Historian,* he fell out of favor with the emperor, who sentenced him to castration. Men were expected to commit suicide rather than submit to such a humiliating penalty. Sima Qian accepted his punishment so that he could finish his book. "I shall deposit it in the [imperial] archives," he wrote to a friend. "If it may be handed down to men who will appreciate it, and penetrate to the villages and great cities, then though I should suffer a thousand mutilations, what regret would I have?"

In the first century A.D., historian Ban Gu picked up where Sima Qian had left off. His *Han shu,* or *History of the Former Han,* covered the events of the early Han dynasty. Ban Gu had his own troubles with authority. Suspicious of the historian's motives, Han emperor Ming had him arrested. But this writer's story had a happy ending. The emperor examined Ban Gu's manuscript and found that it did not contain any criticisms of his rule. After that, he not only released the scholar but appointed him to the prestigious post of court historian. Ban Gu died in A.D. 92. His sister Ban Zhao continued his work, completing the Han history.

The Invention of Printing

The texts of Sima Qian, Ban Gu, and other early writers were slowly and painstakingly copied by hand. Then, in the eighth century A.D., the Chinese invented printing. Early printers carved characters and illustrations in raised symbols on large wooden blocks. They inked the blocks, then pressed sheets of paper against them to print the text. The printed sheets were sewn together into a book.

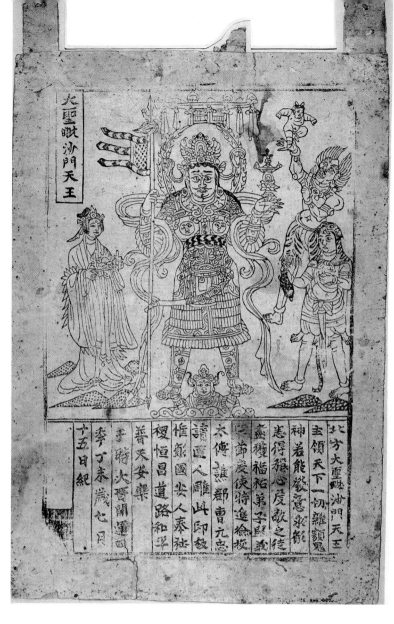

This is one of the earliest dated prints made in ancient China. The central figure is Vaishravana, a popular Buddhist god known as the Guardian of the North.

Printing made books more widely available. That led to an increase in literacy. For the first time people from all levels of society could read the ancient chronicles, poetry, Confucian classics, and Daoist and Buddhist texts. In time the invention of printing would introduce people all over the world to the glorious history and achievements of China's ancient civilization.

Chapter IX

THE LEGACY OF ANCIENT CHINA

By the nineteenth century, China's system of government had become outdated. The Sons of Heaven clung to old traditions, refusing to adapt to the changing world. In 1912 Chinese revolutionaries forced the last emperor to step down. Two thousand years of imperial rule had come to an end.

The revolutionaries set up a republic. Years of unrest and civil war followed. In 1949 the remnants of the republican government retreated to the island of Taiwan, and mainland Communists proclaimed the founding of the People's Republic of China.

Although the Chinese empire ended, its accomplishments have survived. Every time we read a newspaper, go to school, or walk down a city street, we encounter ideas and inventions from ancient China. In this book we have taken a brief look at some of the early inventions, including the iron plow, silk, lacquer, and paper. In later imperial times China gave the world an incredible assortment of innovations. Among these were kites, matches, stirrups, umbrellas, toilet paper, the mechanical clock, **porcelain**, parachutes, hang gliding, printing, paper money, fireworks, and gunpowder. The Chinese also were responsible for important advances in engineering, industry, astronomy, and mathematics. Some of their inventions made everyday life a little easier. Others changed the world.

Today people all over the world continue to enjoy the beauty and variety of ancient Chinese craft work, calligraphy, painting, and poetry. Many have found inspiration in ancient Daoism's message of simplicity and harmony with nature. Traditional Chinese medicine also has gained increasing acceptance in the outside world. Modern doctors have found that age-old treatments such as acupuncture and herbal remedies are sometimes as effective as Western medicine, with fewer side effects.

Perhaps the greatest legacy of ancient China is modern China. This vast land is one of the world's great powers, with the largest population of any nation on earth. The Chinese people are the heirs to the world's oldest continuous civilization. Many of their cultural traditions reach back to the days of the Sons of Heaven.

The Chinese still call their land Zhongguo, or the "Middle Kingdom." For many years after the end of the empire, the traditional view of Zhongguo as the center of the civilized world kept China isolated from other nations. Debate between isolationists and those who favor closer relations with the outside world still continues. However, in recent times Communist China has become more open to tourism, diplomacy, and trade.

Today exhibitions of treasures from ancient Chinese tombs travel the globe. Millions of tourists visit China's ancient and modern cities each year. Outsiders now have a chance to cruise the Grand Canal and retrace the paths blazed by early Chinese travelers along the Silk Road. They can stand before the throne of the last emperor and climb the holy mountain of Taishan. Reviewing the ranks of Qin Shi Huangdi's terra-cotta warriors, they come face-to-face with China's brilliant past.

Chinese herbal medicines and other remedies from ancient times are still used today in China and around the world.

Confucius is born.

Confucius's disciples complete the *Analects*, a collection of his teachings.

Qin Shi Huangdi dies and is buried near present-day Xi'an.

551 B.C. c. **480** B.C. c. **250** B.C. **221** B.C. **210** B.C. **202** B.C.

The Warring States period begins.

Qin Shi Huangdi unifies the Chinese empire.

Liu Bang's rebel army overthrows the Qin.

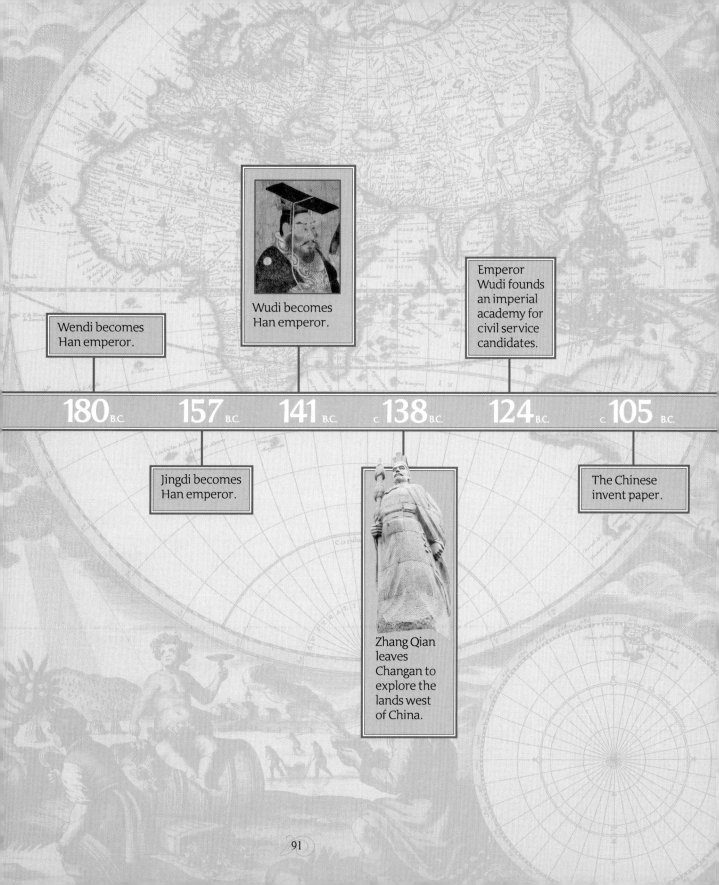

Wudi becomes Han emperor.

Wendi becomes Han emperor.

Emperor Wudi founds an imperial academy for civil service candidates.

180 B.C. **157** B.C. **141** B.C. c. **138** B.C. **124** B.C. c. **105** B.C.

Jingdi becomes Han emperor.

The Chinese invent paper.

Zhang Qian leaves Changan to explore the lands west of China.

Chinese engineers build the world's first suspension bridge in the Himalayan Mountains of southern Asia.

Ban Zhao completes the *Han shu,* or *History of the Former Han,* begun by her brother Ban Gu.

Scholars complete the first Chinese dictionary.

| 92 B.C. | c. 25 B.C. | A.D. 25 | c A.D. 80 | c A.D. 100 | A.D. 121 | A.D. 132 |

Sima Qian completes *Shiji,* or *Records of the Grand Historian*.

Emperor Guang Wudi restores the Han dynasty after 15 years of rebellion and moves the capital east, from Changan to Luoyang.

The "endless chain" irrigation device is invented.

Zhang Heng invents the seismograph.

Li Bo is born.

Mongol invaders under Genghis Khan destroy Zhongdu (modern-day Beijing).

• Beijing

▲ Mt. Langya

Marco Polo writes *The Travels of Marco Polo.*

A.D. **701**   C.A.D. **900**   A.D. **1215**   A.D. **1279**   C.A.D. **1300**   A.D. **1912**

The Chinese invent porcelain.

Kublai Khan and the Mongols complete the conquest of China.

Chinese revolutionaries force the last emperor, Puyi, to give up the throne.

Ban Gu

A.D. 32–92

Ban Gu was a Han scholar, poet, and historian. His father, Ban Biao, was a government official who began work on a supplement to Sima Qian's *Records of the Grand Historian.* After Ban Biao's death, Ban Gu used the records compiled by his father to write the *Han shu,* or *History of the Former Han,* which became a model for later imperial histories.

Ban Zhao

c. A.D. 49–120

Ban Zhao was the younger sister of the historian Ban Gu. She completed her brother's work on the *Han shu* after his death. Ban Zhao also wrote poetry and essays. Her most famous work was *Nujie,* or *Lessons for Women,* a book of rules for proper feminine behavior.

Chao Cuo

200–154 B.C.

Chao Cuo was a government official and agriculture expert who served as an adviser to Han emperors Wendi and Jingdi. His ideas for improving farming methods and tools made the work of peasant farmers easier and more productive.

Confucius

551–479 B.C.

Confucius was a philosopher whose teachings were the basis of Confucianism. He spent much of his life traveling around China, instructing a small band of followers. After his death his disciples put his writings into words in an influential work called the *Analects.* His Chinese name was Kong Fuzi.

Ko Hung

A.D. **283–343**

Ko Hung was a Chinese alchemist whose ideas are recorded in the *Pao P'u Tzu.* Ko Hung's text includes secret Daoist charms and spells, as well as scientific procedures and formulas for making precious metals and elixirs believed to prolong life.

Kublai Khan

A.D. **1215–1294**

Kublai Khan was the founder of China's Yuan dynasty. His grandfather Genghis Khan had founded the Mongol empire and conquered most of northern China. After Kublai became Mongol emperor in A.D. 1260, he completed the conquest of China and built a magnificent capital at Beijing. The splendors of his court became famous across Europe through the writings of the Venetian merchant-traveler Marco Polo.

Laozi

Sixth-century B.C.

Laozi was a philosopher who is said to have written the *Dao De Jing,* the text that formed the basis of Daoism. Modern scholars disagree over when Laozi lived and whether he actually wrote the classic text.

Li Bo

A.D. **701–762**

Li Bo was one of imperial China's most famous and influential poets. He wrote some 1,100 poems celebrated for their imagination and expressiveness. His themes included the joys of nature, love, friendship, and wine. He is also known as Li Po or Li Bai.

Liu Bang

247–195 B.C.

Liu Bang was the founder of China's Han dynasty. Born a peasant, he became a low-ranking government official, in charge of a small band of soldiers. Over time his forces grew into an army, and he led a successful uprising against the Qin rulers. His imperial title was Gaodi, or "High Emperor."

Liu Sheng

died 113 B.C.

Liu Sheng was the son of the fourth Han emperor, Jingdi. He ruled the state of Zhongshan, in northern China. Historical accounts portray him as a man who preferred the pleasures of food, wine, music, and women over the drudgery of politics.

Qin Shi Huangdi

259–210 B.C.

Qin Shi Huangdi was China's first emperor and founder of the Qin dynasty. He unified the empire and established many institutions that would last throughout China's imperial age. These included a strong central government, a single form of the written language, a common currency, and a standardized system of weights and measures.

Sima Qian

146–86 B.C.

Sima Qian was a Han historian and author of China's first historical record, a 130-chapter work called *Shiji,* or *Records of the Grand Historian.* When Sima Qian defended a general who had fallen out of favor with Emperor Han Wudi, he was sentenced to castration and was expected to commit an "honorable" suicide rather than submit. However, the historian accepted the punishment so that he could finish his ambitious project.

Wudi

156–87 B.C.

Wudi was the fifth Han emperor, under whose rule China enjoyed a long period of growth and prosperity. Han Wudi nearly doubled the size of the empire through conquests and alliances. He also established an imperial academy to train future government officials in the Confucian classics.

Zhang Heng

A.D. 78–139

Zhang Heng was a Han scientist, mathematician, and geographer. He served as imperial astrologer and invented the first seismograph, a device for detecting earthquakes. He was also a celebrated poet, painter, and historian.

Zhang Qian

died 113 B.C.

Zhang Qian was a famous Han explorer. In 138 B.C. he was sent out into the unknown lands west of China by Emperor Wudi, on a mission to build diplomatic alliances. He brought back the first reliable information on the lands of central Asia, and his discoveries helped to establish trade along the Silk Road.

archaeologists scientists who study the physical remains of past cultures to learn about human life and activity

astrologers scientists who predict human affairs based on the supposed influence of the stars and planets

astronomers scientists who study the sun, moon, stars, and other heavenly bodies

Bactrian camels Central Asian camels with two humps. The other species of camel, the dromedary, has one hump and comes from Arabia and North Africa.

bureaucracy a complex government system with many levels of departments and officials

caravan a group of people and pack animals who travel together across a desert or through dangerous lands

characters symbols used in writing

concubines the "secondary wives" of an emperor or other high-ranking man. A concubine had lower status and fewer rights than the principal wife.

crossbow a powerful weapon consisting of a bow mounted across a wooden stock. The arrow is released by pulling a trigger and has enough force to pierce armor.

dynasty a line of rulers who pass down their authority from generation to generation

elixir a mixture of ingredients, especially one that is believed to change base metal into gold or to prolong life

enlightenment in Buddhism, the blissful state of total knowledge and freedom from desire

imperial relating to an emperor or empire

inscriptions words written or engraved on stone, metal, or another hard surface

marquis a high-ranking nobleman of ancient China who was granted rights over a large area of land

millet a cereal grass grown for its grain, which is ground into meal or flour

Mongol a member of a group of nomadic peoples from Mongolia, north of China, who created the world's largest land empire in the thirteenth century A.D.

nomadic wandering from place to place, often with herds of grazing livestock

oracles priests who were believed to communicate with the spirit world. Gods or spirits spoke through an oracle to answer questions and forecast the future.

porcelain a very fine type of pottery that was invented in China around A.D. 900. Porcelain is sometimes called "china."

regent someone who temporarily governs in place of a ruler who is too young or weak to take command

rudder a flat piece of wood or metal attached to the rear of a boat and used in steering. The rudder was invented in China around the second century A.D.

sunspots dark spots on the sun's surface, caused by solar magnetic storms

supernova the explosion of a very large star

suspension bridge a bridge that has a roadway suspended on ropes or cables

terra-cotta a kind of baked clay used in statues, pottery, and other objects

topographical showing the shapes and forms of the land

tribute a payment given by one ruler or country to another as a sign of respect and submission

zithers stringed musical instruments

Books

Allison, Amy. *Life in Ancient China.* The Way People Live series. San Diego, CA: Lucent Books, 2001.

Beshore, George. *Science in Ancient China.* New York: Franklin Watts, 1998.

Clements, Jonathan. *Chinese Life.* Early Civilizations series. Hauppage, NY: Barron's Educational Series, 2000.

Hall, Eleanor J. *Ancient Chinese Dynasties.* World History series. San Diego, CA: Lucent Books, 2000.

McNeese, Tim. *The Great Wall of China.* Building History series. San Diego, CA: Lucent Books, 1997.

Martell, Hazel Mary. *Imperial China: 221 B.C. to A.D. 1294.* Looking Back series. Austin, TX: Raintree Steck-Vaughn, 1999.

O'Connor, Jane. *The Emperor's Silent Army: Terracotta Warriors of Ancient China.* New York: Viking, 2002.

Patent, Dorothy Hinshaw. *The Incredible Story of China's Buried Warriors.* Frozen in Time series. New York: Marshall Cavendish, 2000.

Steele, Philip. *Step into the Chinese Empire.* New York: Lorenz Books, 1998.

Williams, Brian. *Ancient China.* New York: Viking, 1996.

Williams, Suzanne. *Made in China: Ideas and Inventions from Ancient China.* Berkeley, CA: Pacific View Press, 1996.

Organizations and Online Sites

Ancient China
http://emuseum.mankato.msus.edu/prehistory/china/index.html

The Minnesota State University's online EMuseum offers lots of information on the history of China, from prehistoric through late imperial times.

The Art of China
http://pasture.ecn.purdue.edu/~agenhtml/agenmc/china/china.html

This colorful site explores arts and crafts, music, language, foods, astrology, historic sites, and other aspects of the culture of ancient and modern-day China.

China the Beautiful
http://www.chinapage.com/main2.html

This collection of "quick links" covers a wide variety of topics related to China's cultural heritage, including art, poetry, literature, painting, philosophy, religion, science, history, and more.

Indianapolis Museum of Art
4000 Michigan Road
Indianapolis, IN 46208
http://www.ima-art.org/

Galleries scheduled to open in early 2006 at the Indianapolis Museum of Art will span more than six thousand years of Asian art. Visit the museum's Web site for photos of items from the Chinese Art collection.

Metropolitan Museum of Art
1000 Fifth Avenue
New York, New York 10028-0198
http://www.metmuseum.org/collections/co_learn_more.asp?dep=6#a

The Metropolitan Museum has the largest collection of Asian art in the Western world. Its Web site offers photos and descriptions of fifty items from the collection, including ancient Chinese paintings, calligraphy, sculpture, and burial goods. The Timeline of Art History explores dozens of topics related to Chinese art and culture.

Norton Museum of Art
1451 S. Olive Avenue
West Palm Beach, FL 33401
http://www.norton.org/collect/frameset.htm

The Chinese collection at the Norton Museum includes sculpture, ceramics, bronze vessels, jewelry, and many other treasures from pre-historic and imperial times. Visit the Web site for thumbnail photos of a selection of works.

Secrets of Lost Civilizations: China Bridge
http://www.pbs.org/wgbh/nova/lostempires/china

This companion site to the PBS television program "China Bridge" uses words and pictures to document the modern-day re-creation of a Chinese bridge known only from an ancient painting. Click on "Bridge the Gap" for an interactive game that tests your bridge-building skills.

Silk Road Encounters
http://www.askasia.org/teachers/Instructional_Resources/FEATURES/SilkRoad

Explore the geography, history, and culture of trade along the Silk Road.

About the Author

Virginia Schomp has written more than fifty titles for young readers on topics including dinosaurs, careers, biographies, and American history. Her writings on cultures of the past include *The Ancient Greeks, Japan in the Days of the Samurai,* and *The Italian Renaissance,* as well as *Ancient Mesopotamia,* another title in the People of the Ancient World series. She is most intrigued by the "story" in history—the writings and remembrances that bring alive the struggles, sorrows, hopes, and dreams of people who lived long ago. Researching ancient China gave her an opportunity to explore some of the wonderful literature of that culture and to rediscover some old favorites among Chinese romantic poetry and the perennial wisdom of the *Dao De Jing.*

Ms. Schomp earned a Bachelor of Arts degree in English Literature from Pennsylvania State University. She lives in the Catskill Mountain region of New York.